The Lost Letters

by Agnes Just Reid

The Lost Letters
by Agnes Just Reid

Published by:

Cedar Creek Press
11544 W Jenilyn Ct
Boise ID 83713

ISBN 0-9653539-1-5
Copyright 2000, 2006, 2021, Presto Preservation Association

All rights reserved. No part of this book may be reproduced or transmit- ted in any form or by any means, electronic or mechanical, including photocopying, recording or by any information storage and retrieval system without written permission from the publisher, except for the inclusion of brief quotations in a review.

Introduction

by Rick Just
Great Grandson of Emma Thompson Just

Letters of Long Ago, by Agnes Just Reid, is a classic pioneer story that has endured for nearly a century at this writing, finding new fans with each of its four printings in 1923, 1936, 1973, and 1997. Reid used letters as a literary device to tell the story of her mother, Emma Thompson Just, who came to Idaho in 1863. The letters Emma wrote to her father, George Thompson, had been lost. Their re-creation for the book was essentially the recording of an oral history. Emma Thompson Just approved each of the "letters" as they came off the typewriter, so we have reasonable assurance of their accuracy so far as memory would allow.

A year after the death of Agnes Just Reid, her niece, Mabel Bennett Hutchinson, who had illustrated the original book, found a similar manuscript. Although much shorter than the original, it still features the simple yet powerful writing of the first, again using the device of letters from Emma to tell the story of her earlier life. This time the letters were written to her "Cousin Lucy." They are published here for the first time as *The Lost Letters,* by Agnes Just Reid.

How well does this account tell the early story of Emma Thompson Just? It is questionable whether Emma ever saw this manuscript. She died November 8, 1923, before she ever got a chance to hold Letters of Long Ago in her hands. Did Agnes Just Reid write both manuscripts before her mother's death, choosing to publish only the years from 1870 to 1891? I believe that is unlikely. *Letters of Long Ago* reads like a book complete unto itself from beginning to end, as does *The Lost Letters*. It is far more likely that Reid was encouraged by the first book's success and set out to write another about her mother's early life. Why it was never published is anyone's guess. Perhaps the author did not think it was up to her standards. Maybe she thought it was simply too short.

If her daughter wrote the manuscript after the death of Emma Thompson Just, it did not have the benefit of her review. Keeping that in mind, it is still an important record. Agnes Just Reid knew her mother as well as any daughter could. She had access to letters and diaries that would help her fill in the blanks. Most of all, the book is believable because Emma was an uncommonly frank woman.

The Lost Letters completes Emma's story. It is a story of agony and achievement, pride and pain. Through her richly talented daughter, Emma speaks to us from across a century when Idaho was barely an idea.

The Found Manuscript

Mabel Bennett Hutchinson distributed copies of the manuscript she found to family members in 1982. The manuscript was untitled. Hutchinson called it Letters of Longer Ago. The following is from her introduction for the family.

To the descendants of George and Emma Bennett, I feel that the publication of these letters is invaluable. This story of the hardships born by the early pioneers is clearly expressed here and should be a reminder of our precious heritage.

The letters written by my Aunt Agnes Just Reid were dictated to her by her mother, Emma Thompson Bennett Just. They are addressed to "Cousin Lucy" in London, England. I don't know when Agnes wrote the manuscript, but she sent the carbon copies to me sometime in the early 1930s. Emma died November 8, 1923, so Agnes could have written them sometime before her mother's death. This manuscript should have preceded Letters of Long Ago, first published in

1923, but it did not. No one seems to know just when Agnes wrote these letters. The previous book begins in December 1870, after Emma had received her legal divorce papers from George Bennett, and had married Nels Just. Agnes sent the carbon copies of her manuscript to me after I left Idaho and was living in Riverside, California. I have no record of the date she sent it to me. I had carelessly put the copy with some old records and papers I had written in college. I had completely forgotten that I had it, or that it existed. It was 1977, after my husband died, when I was rummaging through some old files that I came across the manuscript.

For me, this was an exciting experience.

Here before my eyes were my Bennett "roots." It seemed like fate that these old yellowed and faded sheets of typing paper had surfaced after all these years! When I received this carbon copy, I read it, put it aside, and unfortunately put little value on it, thinking that the original would be preserved and perhaps published. But my faded copy seems to be the only manuscript in existence. Agnes' sons did not know of her having written it, and the original has never been found. Perhaps Agnes destroyed it. Now that these aged and faded pages have followed me for more than forty years, I feel that they must be preserved.

Mabel Bennett Hutchinson, 1982

Agnes Just Reid

Ogden, Utah Territory
January 21, 1860

Dear Cousin Lucy:

Today I am ten years old and for my birthday mother is going to let me write to you. Oh, I have wanted to write to you ever since we came to America. There are so many things that I want you to know, and when my father writes to your mother, he never tells the things that I want him to. Perhaps if mother would write, she would say the things I want her to, but poor dear does not know how to write or to read. I think it is a shame for it would give her something to do when she is so lonesome away out here, so far from her people.

Still, there is not much for one to read.

I have been to school for three months, and there were only half a dozen books that had to be passed around to a room full of children.

But I have tried hard to learn to write and to spell so that I can tell you about this new world.

Each day since I left England and you, I have wished that you had come with us. It would have been so much fun to have you with me--two of us to do everything that I have had to do alone. You are the only person back there that I can remember, and the only thing I can remember of the place is that you lifted me up to pick some grapes. Mother tells me now it was the grape arbor, and it may have been the day we were leaving.

You know, perhaps, that my sister died crossing the ocean and my brother at Saint Louis after we landed. I can only remember them the least little bit, but I wish they might have come on with us.

There is only one thing I can remember about the trip over the ocean. I could walk straight in the ship, but my uncle, being so tall, swayed around and almost fell. I thought it funny. My mother tells me that we were six weeks on the water, and we were almost shipwrecked.

We came across the plains more easily than some did. At Fort Leavenworth, my father found a man who was too sick to drive his team of oxen, so we came with him. Mother tells me we were months making the trip, but it just seems like a day or two to me. Just three things of the trip I can remember. The wagon train had to stop to let a great herd of buffalo pass. I can see them now how the long strings of black could be seen for miles, and then as they came closer, we could see their shaggy coats and the white dust flying up from the trails they were cutting with their feet.

Another thing was an accident. One night we traveled late, and a woman fell from one of the wagons and was run over. I think she died that night, but I can remember how she looked when they picked her up.

Then I remember some Indians who came and looked into our wagon and begged for things. Their faces were so painted that I felt a little afraid, and I was glad when the sick man told my mother to give them anything they wanted so they would go away.

We reached Utah in November. Our first home was a chicken coop about ten feet wide and twelve feet long, made of logs and with no floor except the dirt. My mother cried so much, but my father and I were happy. Being a shoemaker, he soon found work to do and was glad to take anything for pay, so we always had something to eat.

There came a time when things to eat were not easy to get. In 1856 the grasshoppers took everything. Not a seed that was planted was allowed to mature. I have seen my father go to work with nothing for breakfast but a few sour dock greens, thickened with what flour my mother could shake from the flour sack.

One thing nice for us, we had a cow between two families. So nearly all summer, my mother would take a drink of milk and lie down. Once I came to her there and told her I was too sick to play. She asked me how I felt, and I told her I thought I'd be better if I had a piece of bread to eat. She looked at me with tears streaming down her face and said: "My child, my only one, I have never begged, but I'll have to go now." She went to a friend who gave her part of a loaf of very poor bread, the flour was so dark because sunflower and other weed seeds were ground with the wheat, but it was the best thing I ever tasted. The next spring, we ate the meat of cattle that had drowned during the winter, and as soon as things began to grow, we children dug segos on the hillsides. The sego is a tiny juicy vegetable, something like an onion but is mild to eat. I have dug them with a sharp stick until the skin was worn off the front of me where the stick pressed.

After all I have told you, you will be glad that you did not come with us, but it is hard to tell you of the things that make us glad we came. I cannot tell you how it makes me feel every time I see the sunrise over these mountains. Mother always talks of going home, but I know that it would never be home to me without the hills. It seems to me I could not stand to look and look and see nothing but space.

I have many friends here, and we have such good times together, and now I have a baby brother named George, born the year the grasshoppers took our crops. So I'll not be lonesome now, for wherever I go there will be someone to go with me.

Mother says I must not use any more paper this time, so next time I write, I shall try and tell of more happy times.

Your loving cousin,
Emma

Agnes Just Reid

South Weber, Utah Territory
July 6, 1862

My dear Cousin Lucy:

We have moved again. This is only five miles from our old home at Ogden, and we have a little piece of land so that we have things growing, and I think my mother feels happier.

Poor mother, she is often unhappy. Just about the time she makes friends and feels like we were going to have a home, we do something else. A few years ago, there came an order from the church leaders for some of the settlers to move south to a part of Utah Territory known as Dixie. My people were among the ones chosen to go. It was an adventure for my father and me, but mother dreaded it and was unhappy all the time. There were so many wonderful things to see, but I don't think mother ever saw any of them. Some wagon made a song about this move south. This is the way some of it goes:

"I hitched up Jim and Baldy
And to Dixie I did start,
To leave my home in Cottonwood
It almost broke my heart;
The reason why they called on me
I really do not know,
But to hoe the cane and cotton
To Dixie I must go.

"As Betsy was a walking
Says I to her, take care,
When all of a sudden
She struck a prickly pear,
She began to yell and holler
As loud as she could bawl,
Saying if I was back in Cottonwood,
I wouldn't come at all."

Many like Betsy, wished themselves back and in the fall, we were permitted to return to our homes.

This is a great place to live. So many things to do.

My mother says that in England only the rich have ponies to ride, but here almost the poorest have ponies they get from the Indians and what fun it is to ride. I am going to have one of my own soon, but I have learned to ride the horses that belong to other children. It is the most fun in the world. I love horses, and one time I had a ride on a splendid horse. His name was "Charger." Isn't that the best name you ever heard for a horse? It was years ago.

My mother says I was only eight years old. Early one morning, a man came riding up to our house. That was when we lived out by ourselves on what is called Ogden Bench. He had gold buttons on his coat, gold cord on his hat, and gold on his saddle. I had never seen such a grand man, but the horse was even grander. He was sorrel, and his coat glistened as if it had been made of fine satin. While the man was in the house talking to my father, I made friends with the horse and, finding that he liked me, I led him to a fence and climbed on his back. I had gone quite a distance when I heard some very frightened men calling for me. I had to go back, but l did not want to. My father was both frightened and pleased, but the grand man said: "It is a wonder Charger did not take you right to the command. He knows nothing about children, perhaps never saw one before." My father knew by the uniform that the man was a major from soldier camp.

My father and I are usually the best friends, but kind as he is, he gave me a whipping once that neither he nor I can ever forget. He was doing some work for a neighbor, and his team of oxen had strayed in the night, so while he ate his breakfast, I was to hunt them. As I passed down the road toward the range, my cousin Folly was in the watermelon patch trying to see if any were ripe. She was six, and I was eight, so I had to tell her which were nearest ripe. We must have thumped a good many for the first thing I knew, I could hear my father calling, and when I got back to the road, I could see him coming, walking very fast, and grabbing sunflower switches as he came. The sunflowers were all grown tall and were either in full bloom or in bud. You can scarcely think of anything that could hurt more. He whipped me with them all the way home. When one handful wore out, he got another, and my poor body, which only had two thin garments on it, was bruised and bleeding by the time I ran to my mother for help.

Mother only said, "You've been a naughty girl, don't come to me for help."

The whipping was not so bad, though bad enough, but as soon as my father realized what he had done, he was the most heart-broken man you ever saw, and to see him cry made me feel worse than the whipping. He never went to work that day. He could do nothing but grieve over sinfulness.

Because it is the only whipping he ever gave me, I shall always remember him as the kindest of parents, but it would have been so much better for us both if I had gone after the oxen.

Things are not so hard for us now. I've even had a pretty white dress. My mother sews so well because of the years she worked with a tailor that I have many things that other children cannot have. She made me a pretty white dress with tucks and tucks in the skirt and some little red shoes to go with it. She made the tops of cloth, and father put the soles on. I was pleased with them, but the very first time I went to Sunday school wearing them, there were some sheep in the road, and I thought I'd scare them. One big fellow, with horns, did not get scared at all, and the first thing I knew, all of my pretty things were being tramped in the dust.

Another time I wore the dress, someone gave me a watermelon, and it was heavy, so I carried it home in my dress. When I got home, all the lovely tucks that my mother had put in were gone. Father says I am a "Tom Boy" and says he is going to get me a buckskin dress. I think that would be all right. I do not care much for things to wear anyway. Once at school I had trouble about my clothes. My father had picked up two old shirts that some soldiers had thrown away. One had an arm and hammer design, and the other had anchors. It took them both to make a dress for me then the children laughed at the dress. Some of the children were wearing shoes that my father had never been paid for making, so I felt very sad, but I have better dresses now, so I shall soon forget the ones that caused trouble.

I wish you were here. We'd get some ponies and ride to the top of one of these mountains. They seem to reach right up to the sky and have snowbanks on them all year-round.

Write soon. My mother sends her regards.

Your loving cousin,

Emma

Agnes Just Reid

Soda Springs, Idaho Territory
December 11, 1864

My dear Cousin Lucy:

Much has happened since I wrote to you last, and I have been so busy having a good time that I hardly have time to write. More than ever now, I wish you were here with me.

For more than a year now, we have been in another new home. A number of families who were dissatisfied in Utah came here to Idaho with Military Escort.[1] I wonder if you know what that means. Well, it simply means soldiers, wonderful fellows in blue suits with brass buttons. (I used to think they were gold buttons.) The country is full of Indians so that it is unsafe for a few families to try to make a new settlement, and the United States Government sent this company of soldiers to protect us.

We came in the spring, and most of our journey was made up the valley of the Bear River. It was a trip I shall always remember, for the hillsides were so green and flower-covered and the river so deep and blue. We are living now almost on the bank of the same river where there are many mineral springs which give it the name of Soda Springs. We had not been there long when a party of us young folks discovered an especially good spring not far from our settlement. People who have tasted the famed waters of other countries say it is as fine as any. I don't think anyone had ever tasted it before the men took the sod away and opened up the source. They have named it "Ninety Percent Spring."

The mountains are not so steep and rugged as Ogden's, but it is a beautiful spot. There are heavily timbered hills stretching away to the south and beyond them, mountains that are also timbered. From these forests have come homes for us all. The first summer was spent mostly in building a log house for each family and quarters for the soldiers.

In the lower stretches nearer the river, there are miles and miles of cedar that are very ornamental and supply us all the fuel we need. It truly is a favored spot. The Creator must have designed it just for this little band: logs to build our houses, firewood to keep us warm, health-giving waters to drink, streams full of fish, and mountains full of game.

I live the gayest life. Parties of young folks go horseback riding, sleigh riding, and fishing. There is always fun and adventure. There are many good singers among the soldiers, and how often we ride through the cedars and make them echo with our voices.

The first Fourth of July we were here, there were no buildings, so the soldiers found a place where the grass was very smooth, and over it they stretched a large canvas and nailed it down tightly. On this we danced, and what a gay party it was with the light of the campfires and the light of the stars to help in choosing partners.

Now we dance two or three times a week in the soldiers' big dining room. It has a big fireplace, and there are many fiddlers among the soldiers and settlers, so all goes merrily. My father was right when he called me a "Tom Boy" for I surely love to fish and there is not a man in the camp who can catch more than I can. We usually go in couples, and I can nearly always land more than my companion. Sometimes we go about twenty miles out to another stream called the Blackfoot River.

The fishing is better there. You can pull them out as fast as you can drop your hook in. When we get too many at once, we dry and smoke them for winter use.

I have seen one fishing tragedy. One of the oldest men was out fishing with me, and in climbing over rocks along the river, one very large one was loosened and fell on his leg.

Of course, it was badly crushed, and we had no doctor in the settlement, but the hospital steward knew something of such things, and he set the bone so that it did a very good job of healing. My mother and I took care of the poor fellow until he was well, and when he went to Salt Lake, he sent me a lovely locket and chain. It is the first bit of jewelry I ever had, and I am very proud of it. I wish you could see it.

No one here is really in want. You see, the soldiers have their regular income, and there is no place here to spend money, so if they see the settlers in need, they help out. Many of the girls have coats made from blankets that have been issued to the soldiers and made up by the camp tailor. It causes much merriment sometimes to try and figure out which coats have the same colored stripe and thereby find out which soldier gave a coat to any particular girl.

It is something like a school, so many young folks here together, and it really is an education to the young folks of the settlement, for many of the soldiers are well educated.

You see, they enlisted expecting to go to the seat of war, the war over the freeing of the slaves that was raging in the eastern part of this country. They were sorely disappointed when they were sent here instead, but they seem to be getting over the disappointment. Several of the soldiers have married the settlers 'girls, and it looks as if many more would do the same. They plan on staying on here and building homes after they are discharged from the army.

There is one thing unpleasant about this place. It is very cold. Last year, our very first experience when we reached here on May 22, was to wake up the next morning with several inches of snow on our beds. The nights, even in midsummer, are very cool with frequent frosts. Things do not grow as they did in Utah. One man raised a big patch of turnips last summer, and we young folks made regular trips out there to get them. I think they must be even better than the grapes I can remember in England.

I must not waste more time writing, or I shall be late for some of these good times.

Oh, you asked about the Indians. We see a great many of them here. Sometimes they outnumber the white settlers, two to one, but they are friendly. A few months before we came here, there was a terrible battle, we passed very near the site of it coming here, and many Indians were killed. It has quieted them.[2]

Your happy, loving cousin,

Emma

1. It is interesting to speculate why Agnes Just Reid chose not to detail the reasons for the military escort. Perhaps she thought young Emma would not have done so, even though it was a pivotal incident in her life—an incident in which her father nearly lost his life. The episode that brought the settlers to Soda Springs, commonly known as the Morrisite War, is recounted in Letters of Long Ago in the chapter titled "The Witness Stand."

2. "It has quieted them" is an especially chilling comment here. The battle referred to is known today as the Bear River Massacre, possibly the bloodiest encounter with natives in Western history. More than 250 Indians lost their lives. Because the Civil War was taking place at the same time, history has often overlooked this incident.

Soda Springs, Idaho Territory
April 22, 1865

Dear Cousin Lucy:

Here is a surprise for you. I am married.

My mother says you will be horrified to hear of a fifteen-year-old girl getting married, but I know you would not if you just knew what a fine husband I have. Maybe fifteen is too young, but my husband, George Bennett, is twenty-eight, so if we had waited for me to be older, he would have been older too. Anyway, why should we wait? All of our crowd was getting married. My very best girlfriend, who is also English, married an officer in the same company of soldiers that my husband belongs to just a few months ago.

I knew that George was my soldier from the minute I saw him. You see, in the fall, a different company replaced the company of soldiers that came with us here. I knew he was mine just as soon as I looked them over. Fifteen or fifty, what does it matter when you know all the men in two companies of soldiers and a lot more besides, and there is just one among them all that matters? It must be love. It is love.

I never can understand why he wanted me.

I am the plainest, slimmest slip of a girl, and my skin is brown, almost like an Indian. Mother felt awful about it. She said I was only a child in mind and body. I only weigh seventy-three pounds, so perhaps I am a child in body, but my mind is grown up, or I would not be able to select such a splendid man.

He is an Englishman but has traveled much. He spent several years on the South Sea Islands. Oh, Lucy, he really is an English Gentleman. His father is a playwright. Just think of a little immigrant girl marrying such a man. It seems like a dream or a fairy tale.

And he is so handsome, with dark eyes, broad shoulders, fine carriage, and being a Sergeant in the army, he wears prettier uniforms than the ordinary soldiers.

It was too funny the way he asked me to marry him. He had been taking me to dances for several months, and one night when we were a little later than usual getting home, I said as we quickened our steps: "Our mother will be mad at us for being so late." He said: "Let's have her for 'our mother.'" It took me a long time to understand what he meant, but I gladly agreed to have it that way when I was sure.

We were married at a dance, as everyone has been. It is the only time that people assemble here for all the buildings are very small. The couple who is to be married stands at the end of the hall where an officer in the army performs the ceremony. After that, the dance goes on, and after the dance, the army cooks serve supper to everyone, and shortly after midnight, we go to our homes.

Our new home is one of the settler's cabins that was vacant. We have only a few bits of furniture that people have shared with us, but no princess in her castle was ever happier than I.

I cannot do housework. I have helped my father

instead of my mother, so I don't know anything about the work I have to do. The first time I tried to iron a white starched shirt for my new husband, I had a terrible time. Mother finally had to come and do it all over. I will learn, though, for I may not always have my mother so near to me.

The cooking goes better. I do not know a thing about that either, but George has had some experience in that line, so he helps me. Whatever he does, he does better than anyone.

One of his duties as an orderly Sergeant is making out the muster rolls, which is really the individual record of each man in the company. Each one of these rolls is as large as a good-sized table, and George fills them in. His penmanship is perfect. When he gets one of the rolls finished, it looks fit for framing, for every stroke of his pen adds beauty to it.

I sometimes sit for hours, watching him do those things. His pen moves so gracefully like the brush of an artist, and I gaze in wonderment.

It was hard to leave my mother but not as hard now that they have other children. My brother George is quite a big boy now, and I have a little sister Lizzie, such a darling baby. The name

George has certainly always been with me. It was not enough that my father and brother had the name, I had to marry another George, and to make it still more strange, we were married on George Washington's birthday. That is a special holiday in this country, being the birthday of the first President of the United States.

Life goes on in much the same way it did before our marriage. We go to many dances and for many horseback rides, and there is no one to scold if we are late getting home. If I can't cook, I can still boast that I am a good rider. Whenever there are not enough saddles to go around, I gladly take the horse without a saddle, and it is nothing to ride thirty miles beside those who have saddles. Of course, there are no side saddles to be had, but we get along very well on the men's saddles, as always, of course, riding sideways. A girl would be disgraced to ride like a man.

Some of the soldiers, who have received their discharge from the army, are going on places of their own, hoping to make homes. It is a wonderful place to make such a venture.

Oh, dear, I must stop writing and start to fry the fish. I have a hungry husband who will be home before I know it. I am perfectly happy, even if I do make a few mistakes in housekeeping.

Your joyful cousin

Emma

Agnes Just Reid

Fort Douglas, Utah Territory
December 20, 1865

Dear Cousin Lucy:

Well, you see your wandering cousin has moved again. This time it was not such an adventure, for it meant leaving my father and mother, really leaving them, for the first time in my life. A soldier man is not boss of himself, so when George was transferred here, it meant that we must make another home.

The first night we camped after leaving Soda Springs was by a waterfall, and though the world was full of beauty, it was the saddest night of my life. I don't think I ever went to sleep, I just listened to the falling water all night, and it was the most lonesome sound I have ever heard. I've heard people speak of the music of waterfalls, but this one did not make music for me.

We are settled now in quarters that are provided for the married soldiers, but everything is very different and very strange. The rules of the camp are more rigid here so that George has to be on duty a good deal, and I am lonesome, very lonesome.

There is only one thing I have to take the place of all the old times at Soda Springs. Next to our house is a large empty storeroom, and when the big military band plays, which it does every day, I go into that big room and dance and dance until I forget that I am alone. Guess anyone to see me would think I am crazy, but no one ever does see me, so it is all right.

Sometimes I feel almost like I have come back to Earth after living for a time in paradise. At Soda Springs, we were all like one big family. There were no quarrels, no drunkenness, no bickering at Soda Springs; here, we find all of those things. The Fort is just a short distance from Salt Lake City, and the soldiers go there and get drunk.

Then there is always a quarrel between the people

who are Mormons and the people who are not. The Mormon people are thrifty, industrious people and frown upon anything disorderly, but even they do something that I can never believe is right. The men have more than one wife.

I know now that I had heard my mother speak of it when we lived at Ogden, but it did not mean anything to me then. Now, it means a great deal. I think my mother always feared that my father would take another wife, for I know he used to joke with her about it. I am glad that my husband is not a member of that church, for I know it would kill me if he should ever bring home another wife.

The Mormon people have built a fine theater at Salt Lake, and there are many things given there that are equal to the best given in the States. We go often. Of course, the theater is almost like home to George, and to me it is a perfect fairyland. I hardly dare breathe during a whole performance for fear of missing a word, and sometimes when I go home, I can repeat about half of the parts, and quite frequently, I can learn a song, both words, and melody by hearing it once.

Always at the theater, though, there is that hateful

thought of polygamy. Always in his private box, I see Brigham Young and one of his wives. I am not sure that it is always the same one, but there are awful stories about how many wives he has. Oh, you may not know, but he is the leader of the Mormon Church and a fine-looking man. He has led his people to do wonderful things. When I look at the fine homes, stores, churches, farms, and Salt Lake Theater, I wish my people had stayed on there. They might have been living in comfort now but, oh dear, my father might have had another wife.

I have had one terrible experience since we came here. George has been working in the commissary department since we came here, and a few weeks ago, the commissary burned. In it were hundreds and hundreds of dollars worth of supplies for the soldiers; sugar and coffee and bacon and hams and flour. It all cost such a lot here, so it was an awful thing to lose it.

The next morning, they put my husband and another man in the same department in the guardhouse because of this fire. You know the guardhouse is just like a jail to folks who are not in the army, and I almost went insane. To think they would blame my husband because they lost their supplies. You cannot imagine how I felt. I had to stay alone nights and days then and my father and mother so far away.

Someone finally told me that if I would go to the General, I might get George released. That frightened me even more than staying alone. Why even George, who had been halfway around the world and had met people of every color and creed, was afraid of General Connor.[1] How could I go and see him.

I thought of nothing else for days and decided at last that if it was the only hope of freedom for my poor wronged husband I must go. When I was shown into the General's office, I felt as if I were about to meet the Ruler of the Universe; my heart pounded until I could scarcely see. I cannot remember how he greeted me, but I told him somehow that my husband was in the guardhouse, then he said as kindly as my own father might have said: "Why my child, are you married?" Had he been gruff as I expected, I might have stood it, but when he was so kind, I cried like the child I was. He said: "We'll see what we can do about it." He must have been able to do something for the next day George was released, and we are happy again in our little military home. I shall not be lonesome anymore if they will just leave my husband free.

It will not be long now until George is discharged, and I shall be thankful. Army life is not for married men.

As ever, Emma

1. *It was then Colonel Patrick E. Connor who had earlier led his troops against the Indians in the Bear River Massacre. He was a bitter man by most accounts, disappointed that he had missed action in the Civil War.*

Lincoln Valley, Idaho Territory
October 15, 1866

My dear Cousin Lucy:

Last June, George received his discharge from the army, so we returned to Soda Springs at once. It was a sad homecoming for my brother George had died in April. A terrible epidemic of diphtheria had swept the tiny settlement during the winter and spring, and children were taken from many homes. My mother is heartbroken, and I think she is not well, besides. Poor little mother, this new world has been too cruel to her.

Father promises that he will take her back to England. I think he would like to stay on here, but he is convinced now that she will never be contented. He hopes to get enough money ahead by next year for them to make the trip.

Mother has her heart set on my going, too. Of course, if George wants to go, I shall be glad to, but there is really no reason for our going back and every reason that we should stay on.

We are now in the great Snake River Valley, hundreds, yes thousands of acres of level land stretching for hundreds of miles on either side of the gigantic Snake River. It is a land of promise. Many of the old settlers from Soda Springs are coming here. Our very best friends, F.S. and Nettie Stevens moved the house they had at Soda Springs right down here with them and will rebuild it near the mouth of the Blackfoot River, where it joins the mighty Snake River.

My aunt and uncle, the Highams, were coming out here, so we came with them. We are all located on a little mountain stream called "Lincoln Creek." There are many acres of creek bottom that supply us with feed for our stock.

We have been busy since we came here. We had to build ourselves a house, and my husband, who does everything so well, does not know anything about building houses. In fact, he hardly knows how to drive the oxen, so I feel a great deal more necessary here than I did at Salt Lake. You would perhaps laugh at our house. It is tiny with one door and one window. (The window glass is just a rag). The roof is made of willows, with a layer of grass on top, then mud on top of that.

The only furniture we have is a bed, and I think you would like to hear about it. We bored holes in the logs about two feet up from the floor (the floor is the natural earth), where the head and the foot of the bed should be. We put good strong sticks into these and held them at the outside corner with another forked stick. Across this framework, we laid many willows, thus making an ideal spring.

For the mattress, we have a bed tick filled with the fragrant meadow hay and what bed could be finer. Guess it is too fine, for often George comes in from doing the morning milking and finds me still asleep when he expected to find breakfast ready. I beg him to forgive me, for he must know I am not grown up yet, and children are so sleepy. He never chides me for anything. I've heard that Englishmen sometimes beat their wives, but he has never even spoken an unkind word to me. I am very happy here in the wilderness with the man I love. Salt Lake, with its polygamy and drunken soldiers, is only a memory now. We are surrounded by Indians, but I do not fear them. Not far from us is the great Fort Hall Bottom that is a far-famed winter retreat for the Indians, so this time of year, they pass by the hundreds on their way there.

Our income is very limited. We sell some butter and some milk to people passing along the stage road, and all of our supplies must be brought from Utah, more than a hundred miles away. So when they went for winter provisions, I gave them my new coat that had cost $35 at Salt Lake last year, and they traded it for potatoes.

I have even made soap ready for winter. A can of lye cost one dollar, and to that, I added five pounds of butter that I could have sold at 75 cents a pound and made some lovely soap. It sounds like a lot of money, but we must be clean, and it is not likely that we shall be in actual want, for we have lots of supplies, and game is plentiful.

Your loving cousin,
Emma

Taylor's Bridge,
December 1, 1866

Dear Cousin Lucy:

Well, Lucy, it is getting so I cannot stay in one place long enough to finish a letter.

An offer came for us to come here to a toll bridge and cook for stage passengers at sixty dollars a month. To people who had no money, it sounded very good, so we left our little palace in charge of a bachelor soldier, and for the use of it, he will take care of our oxen and milk cows.

Things are rather pleasant here. Most of the time, I am one lone woman among many men, but often women come by on the stage, so I have a few minutes to chat if they seem inclined to talk, and I am not too busy. We have two regular boarders, and they telegraph ahead so that we know how many to prepare for on each stage.

Every other night the stage comes in sometime between midnight and morning, so we are usually up all night then. George is stock tender, so he must be there to have the horses that are going out in the best of trim and take good care of the tired ones that come in. Unless the roads are particularly bad, they keep to a certain schedule, and it all depends upon the poor horses.

George helps me with the cooking, or perhaps I help him. It is hard to tell just how it is, but I really am learning how to cook from him and my aunt. My aunt is a much better cook and housekeeper than my mother, and this last summer, I have tried to learn from her.

Now that we live right on the stage road, it will be easy for me to get letters and I hope you will write soon.

Your busy, happy cousin,
Emma.

Agnes Just Reid

Helena, Montana Territory
November 30, 1867

Dear Cousin Lucy:

Again, it has been a very busy year for me with very little chance to write. We have moved onto the Territory farther north and are again without definite plans.

We spent the winter at Taylor's Bridge, then kept station for a short time at Ross Fork, not far from our little home in Lincoln Valley. While we were there, my father and mother came from Soda Springs and were ready to start for England. My little sister Lizzie had died that winter, leaving my poor mother again with no one but me. She was so sad and wanted us to go back with them, so we gladly agreed to do it.

We had traded our oxen for a pony team, so George suggested that we go ahead since our horses could make so much better time than my father's oxen and we would meet here at Helena and all be ready to go down the Missouri River together. Getting ready is not much of a task, for they just run the settler's whole outfit right onto a flatboat, and he has his own bed and his own cook outfit the same as he would have to cross the desert.

Helena is quite a flourishing mining town, and the only place we could find to live was a tiny miner's cabin quite a distance up the gulch on which the town sits. It was to be only a very temporary home, but each day I did something to add to the comfort of the travelers when they came. Each day I felt sure they would arrive before another day.

I seldom went to the main part of town. George brought me what few things I needed from the stores, and I did not care to go on the streets. It is by far the roughest place I have seen. Hundreds of miners here, and gambling and drinking is quite the order of the day.

George has never missed a day going down and has watched every outfit that has come in but has never seen anything of my father and mother. He has made inquiries of hundreds of travelers since the time passed for them to come, but no one has seen them along the way.

It is so late now that I know we must have missed them. My parents must be back in England by now. Perhaps they are and are telling you at this minute just how we happened to misunderstand each other. It may be that when they got to the boat, it was ready to start, and they figured that we would be on the next boat or perhaps had gone on ahead. I cannot understand it, though. My father is the kind of man that keeps his word, and when they had promised to meet us at Helena, I think, if he were alive, he would have come.

When I think of such things, my world totters around me. What if they took the wrong road and were overtaken by Indians? I hear of such things often. Or they might even have been murdered by some outlaw of our own race. There are plenty of them, and I know my father was carrying considerable money.

I did not really want to go back to England, but if they had just come here to visit us and we had wished them God-speed, how different it would have been. I feel so alone, and for the first time, this new world seems unkind.

George has found an old acquaintance named Mortimer who is very interesting to us both. He is much older than George and has been an actor all his life. He is here with a stock company. We go often to the theater again and because of this man have met some of the other members of the company. I am scared until I can hardly speak when I meet them, but oh, I love to hear them talk. And they have the most beautiful clothes. I never knew that a woman's dress could be so lovely.

Another thing of interest was the Territorial Fair. Oh, it was a grand affair, and George always insists that I go to things of that sort so that I will not worry so much. He says that father and mother are safely in England by now, and I will soon hear from them.

Oh, how I hope he is right. I started to tell you about the fair. You know, I have always been with the vanguard of civilization and have never seen things grow so. The vegetables displayed at the fair were the most remarkable things I ever saw. This part of Montana is mostly mining, and the climate is not so good but over another divide toward the Pacific is what they call the "Bitter Root Valley," and from there came these pumpkins and squash and cabbages, such as I never believed could grow.

Another item of the fair that was very interesting to me was a women's horse race. I longed to take part in it, but I have no horse to ride now. There were several women who took part in the race but only two who mattered. One was a very much over-dressed
woman with a well-kept horse and fine saddle. I think she lives here in Helena. She was not an especially good rider but had tried to make up in equipment what she lacked inability.

Then there was another woman, a born rider, mounted on a horse that had seen service and on a man's saddle. There was one horse that kept spoiling the race by bolting at a certain place in the track, which was made by men by the hundreds forming a circle. After he had done it several times, the woman with the man's saddle asked the judges to let her ride that bolting horse, and she could make him go through. They consented, and the horse went through and won the race. That is, it looked so to everyone but the judges. They awarded the prize to the woman with the fine horse and the fine riding habit.

As soon as it was announced, a roar of dissatisfaction went up from the miners, and somebody passed a hat around the ring. They raised several hundred dollars in a few minutes, and that woman went out of town that night to her home back in the mountains, riding the finest outfit that could be bought for a woman.

I hope if you see my father and mother that you will give them my love and tell them how deeply I regret that we were separated in this cruel manner.

Your lonely cousin,
Emma

Deer Lodge, Montana
September 22, 1868

Dear Cousin Lucy:

It is hard for me to write. When the word came that my mother had died on her way back to her loved ones, I thought I would go crazy. I know that everyone must lose a mother, but it could have come to me less cruelly. If I had gone with them as we had planned and been with her until the last, I think I could have stood it. If they had visited us here and then gone understanding that we were to stay, it would not be so bad. Or if she could have reached her own home so that she could have been surrounded by her loved ones when the end came, but to die at Liverpool, so near the fulfillment of her dreams, is unbearable to me.[1]

I am so, so alone, so heartbreakingly alone.

No one knows how I need a mother or a father. Since she was never to reach England alive, what a shame they ever started.1 If they had stayed here, my father and I could have comforted each other. Now, I am alone among strangers.

We have moved again, and George has a good job in a livery stable. It is work he enjoys. He really is the bookkeeper, but he does some of the work with the horses, and we can always have horses to ride whenever we want to, so that means a great deal to me. I think I shall like it better here in every way. I never liked Helena. I think I mentioned to you that we have associated with theatrical people a good deal at Helena. They were interesting, intelligent people, and I learned a great deal from them, but they were not good company for George. I hope you will not mention this to my father, for I have even lied to him, my own father, to keep him from knowing, but ever since we left Soda Springs, where there was no drink to be had, George has been drinking.

I do not blame him. He really cannot help it. He formed an appetite for it when he was so young that he cannot remember. His mother used to have brandy sauce and all such delicacies served at her table, and he grew to manhood with a taste for it. Then whenever he is with people who drink, they insist, and wishing to be sociable, he drinks too. The more he drinks, the more talkative he becomes and the more witty things he can think of to say, so they urge him to drink more.

When he has spent most of the night in this manner, they bring him home to me. He is no longer a drunken man but a very sick and repentant one. He promises me by all that is good and holy that he will never touch another drop, and I take care of him like a baby until he is well again. Somewhere during his years in the South Sea Islands, he acquired some kind of chronic diarrhea that is always aggravated by his drinking, so that he really is sick. I love to take care of sick people, and I am not lonesome when I have him with me, but I am always so afraid that sometime he will not get over one of these spells, and I try to beg him never to drink again, but it is no use. When he gets with the same old crowd, he does the same things again.

I have hope now, a precious hope that I am hugging to my heart. (Do not tell my father this either, for it would be one more worry for him). We think that we are going to have a baby. The doctor says that we are, but it seems almost too good to be true, after all this time.

Oh, I want a baby more than I ever wanted anything. I need a baby. I am so lonesome that my heart is breaking from it. Oh, if God will only let me have a baby. I'd like it to be a son, for then his father would be so pleased and proud that he would never drink again, and we would be as happy as we were at Soda Springs. I think I could even become reconciled to the thought that my mother is gone if I had a baby. I have so little to do, but it would be different if I had a baby to care for. Oh, the joy of making little clothes! I can hardly wait for the months to pass.

Because of this hope, I have been so very ill. The doctor says that the worst is over now, but I haven't been able to eat for weeks, and I am so thin and weak.

The mail travels so slowly. My mother had been dead four months before the word reached me, then to please George I went that same evening to the theatre. He said that since it had happened so long before, it was foolish to turn my life into one of mourning. I am glad for his sake that I went, but I never saw nor heard anything. My heart was over the seas.

Dear cousin, I hope that your life may never hold as much unhappiness as mine has in the last year.

Your loving cousin,
Emma

1. Although Emma writes that her mother died before reaching England, she did make it to Liverpool. She died on September 28, 1867, at age 40 at the Walton Workhouse. Her infant daughter, born in Soda Springs on April 1 of that year, died two days later. They were buried together.

Agnes Just Reid

Deer Lodge, Montana
January 21, 1869

Dear Cousin Lucy:

Again, it is my birthday. I am nineteen today, but when I look back upon my experiences of the last few years, it seems to me that I should be ninety. One grows up quickly, then grows old soon in this new world.

I can hardly tell where to begin, for so much has happened to me since I wrote to you last. I told you that we were expecting a baby. Had it not been for the promise of that gift of God, I think I would have ended it all. I couldn't have gone on, but somehow, I could not bring myself to do it. I could have taken my own life gladly. There was no reason for going on, but I could not take the life of my unborn babe.

Everything looked so hopeful when I wrote last. George had a good job. He never needed to be out of work, for he could work at so many different things. Things were rather well for a while, then he began to drink and gamble. Night after night, he never came home. Finally, crazed with drink, he robbed his employer, stole a horse from the stable where he worked, and left town. I found myself deserted by my husband four months before becoming a mother, with the rent unpaid and several hundred dollars of his employer's money gone with him. Of course, he was soon overtaken and is now in jail. Such is the end of the romance between a little immigrant girl and an English gentleman.

Friends took me in. Friends that Providence must have sent. At Soda Springs, there was a Swedish girl who married a soldier and did washing for the soldiers until the time of her husband's discharge. I knew her slightly, but she never danced or rode horseback or any of the foolish things I did, so we were never well acquainted. She and her husband live three miles out of Deer Lodge and sell milk to customers in town. When they heard of my plight, they came and brought me to their home.

They are such hard workers. They get up at three o'clock in the morning to get their milking done in time for the early delivery, then feed calves and haul hay until it is time to milk again. Just the two of them, and she works with him all of the time. They have three little children, and they have had to be neglected shamefully. They never even have their clothes off at night. Just tumble in as they are while their father and mother are still busy with the night chores.

They are the busiest people I have ever known and the kindest. They tell me that I am such a great help to them because I can stay with the children and keep the fire going. They share everything they have with me and even insist upon giving me their bed because it is more comfortable. If I live to be a thousand years old, I can never pay them for all of their kindness. They seem to live just to be kind to me. Each day they try to think of some joke to make me laugh. Oh, they have saved my sanity and perhaps my life. Again, they will have my life in their hands, for they promise to take care of me in my confinement, and I do not want a doctor. I think it would be terrible to have a doctor. I've made them promise that even if I become unconscious, they will not send for one.

Now, this is perhaps the saddest of my tragic story. These good people want me to get a divorce as soon as I am able to go to town after the baby comes. To have a husband in jail is not disgrace enough. I must still ask for a divorce. What would my angel mother say to such a thing? At first, I refused to consider it, but the more they urge me, the more I know they are right. They belong to the Catholic Church, and when a Catholic insists upon divorce, it must be necessary.

I cannot keep from thinking of my baby growing up without a father. What would life have been to me without my father? Oh, how can I do it! How can I do it, yet how can I not do it when these people who love me as their own insist upon it?

Yours with a heavy heart,
Emma

Deer Lodge, Montana.
April 30, 1869

Dear Cousin:

I have my baby, a lovely song, so my heart is full of thanksgiving. Many times, within the last few months, I have felt that I had nothing to live for, but when I heard his first cry, everything changed. I have him, and he is all mine, and I must live for him.

These good people had tried in their simple way to prepare me for the coming of a baby. They had warned me again and again that I would be so sick that I would be sure I was going to die, then when my last breath seemed to be spent, the ordeal would be over.

I did not know anything about the coming of a

baby, and I listened to everything they told me and remembered, but oh, I had no idea it was anything like it is. I don't think the people who warned me had any idea what my experience would be. I took sick Saturday evening and from then on never had one moment's rest until my baby was born Monday morning at about ten. This dear good woman, who brought me to her home, stood over me through two weary nights when she so much needed rest herself. They both neglected their work to care for me, and still, there was so little they could do. They had promised me they would not send for a doctor, but the team was all hitched up, ready to go for one, when it was finally over.

I have promised these friends that the baby shall be baptized in their church, and they shall be his Godfather and Godmother. I am not in sympathy with their belief, but I am not with any other creed, so it seems as little as I can do, when I owe my very life to them, to give them that much satisfaction.

I have gained fast so that I am quite well, much better than I had ever hoped to be again while I was going through those hours of torture.

I am reconciled to the idea of a divorce now, but

no one will ever know what it has cost me. When the baby was three weeks old, his father came to see us. What a supreme moment that should be in every woman's life when the father looks for the first time upon their newborn child, his child, and her child. To me, it was my Gethsemane.

He was just released from jail and came directly to see us without any attempt to make himself more presentable. I have seldom seen him without being clean and well-dressed, so the first sight of him was a shock. Then he had no liquor to bolster his self-respect, so he was heartbroken and repentant. He looked at the baby in his cradle and cried, for never did a newborn baby look more like a father. Then he picked him up and, in his old easy, graceful manner, held him in one arm and reached out the other arm for me. I looked him straight in the eye and shook my head, but God in Heaven spare me from ever having to tear myself to pieces in that manner again. He looked bewildered, and then he realized that the child he married had become a woman.

He came again and brought some little gifts for the baby. This time he had a new suit of clothes, a new hat, a fresh shave and haircut, and a few drinks, so he was a different man. It was much easier for me to follow my convictions when I saw him that way.

The divorce will be a simple matter. I shall not even have to appear in open court. Just a few witnesses to swear that he deserted me, leaving me penniless and expecting a baby. That is all-sufficient, they say.

It is spring here now, and never was spring so welcome. The winter was long and the snow very deep. Now, I often take my baby and the other children, and we find a grassy hillside and stay there in the sun for hours. Despite all I have been through, life is sweet with my baby and the springtime.

I am not going to name the baby for his father. I have decided to call him Fred, that is the middle name of this man in whose home the baby was born, and it is a name I really like.[1]

So we both send our love to you,
Emma and little Fred

[1] Many years later, Fred Bennett would marry the eighth child of John Fredwood and Christina Vaughn on the first day of the new century, January 1, 1900. They would have three children.

Agnes Just Reid

Deer Lodge, Montana
September 15, 1869

Dear Cousin Lucy:

The next time I write, I shall be back in Idaho again. Aunt Jane, the only relative I have this side of England, still lives at Lincoln Valley, and Uncle Joe is coming for me. It must be about three hundred miles from here, but I expect him any day now so that we'll be well toward home before cold weather starts.

I hate to leave these good people. Their home has become like home to me, but I must try to do something for myself. My father writes me that he left a few head of cattle with Aunt Jane, and they are to be mine. Something of my own will give me a feeling of independence, and I may find work of some sort.

I am sure too that I shall be happier away from all the scenes of my old life. I must begin a new life, a life that is to be lived for my little son. Already he has started to influence my decisions. I have told you of our many theatrical friends. One manager and his wife were especially interested in me, and a few times I took some minor part in a play. As soon as these people heard of my plight, they came to see me and offered to give me a home and train me for the stage. They said they were sure that I had talent and would be glad to give my baby and me a home as long as we would accept and pay me small wages until I could earn more. It was a great temptation. I love the theater! I can learn the lines so easily that the work part would just be play, but there is my boy to consider. I want him to have a home. I want him to grow into the kind of a man that his father should have been, so I thanked the good people and told them it was not for me. I wonder, sometimes, if I shall ever regret my decision. It would have been such an easy way to support my boy. I am young, and I might even have attained some degree of fame in this new world where talent is so scarce. Still, I know that If I can have a home, I shall never long for the life of an actress, but if I had gone on the stage, I might sometime have passed a little home with children playing in the yard, and that would have broken my heart.

I have my divorce. I can say it with satisfaction now. My father wrote me what I should have known long ago, which made the divorce much less difficult for me. Perhaps the unkindest thing George did was keep me from seeing my father and mother as they passed through on their way to England. My father writes me that they camped right in the main street of Helena for several days, so instead of George looking for them, as I firmly believed, he was making a point of dodging them. Oh, why didn't I just once walk down the street and find the mother that I was never to see again? I see it all now. He did not want to go back to England and never intended to, but it was easier just to let it appear that he did. Easier for him, I guess, but what a blow to me! Oh, why did he so completely destroy my faith in him and all mankind! I sometimes wonder if I can ever trust even my son after such treatment at the hands of a man.

Still, I wonder, after all this grief and unhappiness, can I really put him out of my life? He was my first love and perhaps my last. I need security and peace of mind even more than love.

The Lost Letters

I wonder what the future holds for me and my little one...

Sadly,

Your cousin, Emma

Agnes Just Reid

Lincoln Valley, Idaho Territory
September 1, 1870

Dear Cousin Lucy:

Forgive me for my seeming neglect. Your letter came to me months ago, but I have been so very busy. My uncle came to Montana and brought me back with him late last fall.

We made the trip safely before the winter began, and my little boy and I have been very comfortable here. So comfortable, yes, and almost happy for with the coming of spring, this quiet, peaceful little valley became a veritable beehive of activity.

The United States Government is building a

Military Post here where a few soldiers will be stationed in case the settlers have trouble with the Indians. Instead of the loneliness I looked forward to, I worked from four in the morning until ten at night and was sometimes too tired to sleep when I had the chance. It has been good for me. The ache in my feet helps me to forget the ache in my heart.

You see, with this rush of people into a country with no resources, we have been able to sell everything we could produce. My aunt and I have milked cows and sold milk and butter to the contractors; we have done washing and mending and sewing, and besides helping with other work, I have baked bread for thirty-five men, the soldiers who require one loaf each a day. I have a tiny stove that will bake four loaves at a time, and I have a sack bearing each soldier's name to put the loaf in as it comes out of the oven so that no one will be forgotten.

It was a good time for me to come here, for I have been able to pay for the expense I have been to my aunt and uncle, but I cannot go on. I cannot bring up my boy in the home of someone else. Aunt Jane has two boys of her own, you know. They are twelve and fourteen, and as my boy grows older, they will tease and spoil him.

Besides, it was just never meant that two families should live in one house.

Now, this will shock you, I imagine. I am going to marry again. It shocks me, for it is the one thing I felt positive I would never do. Even when I wrote you last, I would have been horrified at such a suggestion, but we all have to be governed by circumstances. My circumstances are that I have a son, and I want him to have a home, and I cannot build a home by myself in this wilderness.

This young man was boarding with my aunt when I came from Montana, and she and my uncle both think he is an ideal mate for me.
He was born in Denmark and walked across the plains when he was nine years old with the handcart company. He must have energy enough to make a home when he could walk two thousand miles at that age. He is young, too young it seems to me for the men I have known have all been older, but even so, he is three years older than me in years, but with my baby, I feel so much older than he is.

He will never have the one fault that wrecked my other home. He does not drink and has no patience to associate with anyone who does. He does not even use tobacco.

Though born in the old country, he speaks and reads English very well. He is clean and honest and straightforward and fell in love with me the minute we met, but one thing is lacking. I do not love him. Is it possible to build a home without love? He says that his love is great enough for both of us, but he is only a boy. I have been truthful with him. He knows that I do not care as I should, but he is willing to take me, so I shall do my best to make him happy.

He has our new home all picked out. That is the site of it. About twelve miles from here (I don't believe I told you that the new Fort is to be called Fort Hall, so it will not be Lincoln Valley anymore) is a small river called the Blackfoot. I used to fish on the upper end of it when we lived at Soda Springs. After passing through miles and miles of canyon, it begins to spread out just before it reaches the Snake River Valley and has some good farming land on either side. This Nels Just, who is to be my husband says there is plenty of land there for us and our children and grandchildren.

He thinks he will be able to get water on the land in a few years. Then we shall raise wonderful crops. I have several heads of cows, and he has two good teams of oxen. He has been freighting all summer with them, so he will have quite a little "wedding stake" put by when he gets back from his next trip.

In about November, we expect to make a trip with these oxen to Malad, a place nearly a hundred miles from here, the nearest Justice of the Peace who will marry us. Then we'll begin to make a home out here where there is nothing to begin with but courage. I pray that we may have plenty of that. Our address will be Fort Hall. I shall be looking for a letter with your blessing.

Your loving cousin,

Emma

For the continuation of Emma's story, read
Letters of Long Ago,
by Agnes Just Reid

About the Author

Agnes Just Reid, 1886-1976, was a well- known regional writer during the early 1900s. She authored a column in the Blackfoot, Idaho newspaper for more than 40 years and also had many of her poems published in newspapers, magazines and collections. She is best known for her book, *Letters of Long Ago*, a biography of her mother Emma Thompson Just, first published in 1923, the fourth edition of which is still in print.

About the Cover

Artist Brent Cotton, a great-grandson of Agnes Just Reid, is an award-winning, nationally recognized artist living in the Bitterroot Valley of western Montana. He prefers to paint in the Tonalist/Luminist style made popular in the late 1800s, seeking to create mood-evoking works with a timeless quality.

The cover was one of his early works, done while he was still in high school. His work can be found in many private and corporate collections. Several galleries across the nation represent Brent, and he participates in some of the most prestigious museum exhibitions each year.

www.ingramcontent.com/pod-product-compliance
Lightning Source LLC
Chambersburg PA
CBHW072105290426
44110CB00014B/1835